Praying and Fasting
The Bible Way

Thomas Eristhee

Copyright © 2015 Thomas Eristhee

All rights reserved.

ISBN: 1514380986
ISBN-13:9781514380987

CONTENTS

	Acknowledgments	i
1	Introduction	1
2	Why This Book	3
3	Praying and Fasting Defined	11
4	Develop Faith and Cast Out Devils	15
5	How Important is Fasting?	25
6	The Food Problem	41
7	The Doctrine of Prayer and Fasting	45
8	The Benefits of Fasting	47
9	When Should I Fast?	75
10	Overcoming Temptation in Praying and Fasting	83
11	Fasting Helps Get The Job Done	95
12	Starting The Fast	103
13	Breaking Your Fast	109
14	Put Food Where It Belongs	115
15	Intercession and Prayer	125
16	What A Weapon We Have	133
17	Conclusion	139

ACKNOWLEDGMENTS

I thank the Lord Almighty for the revelation and insights He gave me during the writing of this book. Special thanks also to my wife Midran and my children for their unwavering support and understanding. I am further grateful to all the Pastors of the Pentecostal Assemblies of the West Indies, Saint Lucia.

1
INTRODUCTION

There are many persons in this world who have never given their stomach a rest; not even for one day. They know nothing about fasting. There are many in the church for years who have never even fasted for a day, and for some others, they have never heard about the subject in church.

I believe that we are living in desperate times and desperate measures must be taken if we are going to see a move of God in our family, church, nation and the world. One of the measures that must be taken like the prophet Joel says is that we need to call for serious praying and fasting. The people of God must seek Him in the deepest form of prayer there is, that is prayer and fasting.

I trust as you read this book that the Holy Spirit will burden you to seek Him in prayer and fasting until He brings revival in our homes, churches, nation and the world to the glory of God. I trust also that you will be like the prophetess Anna, as is record in the book of Luke 2:36, 37;

"And there was one Anna, a prophetess, the daughter of Phanuel, of the tribe of Aser: she was of a great age, and had lived with an husband seven years from her virginity;

And she was a widow of about fourscore and four years, which departed not from the temple, but served God with fastings and prayers night and day."

This woman was eighty-four years old yet, the Bible says, she served God day and night in the temple with praying and fasting.

2
WHY THIS BOOK?

There are several reasons for this book on fasting and praying. I remember many years ago while I was still a teenager and a saved for just a few years, I almost ended up at the hospital after I had ended seven days of a total fast. By total, I mean I only consumed water during the seven days. After the seven days, because of the limited knowledge I had on the subject, I stopped the fast, abruptly. At that time we were being encouraged to fast, but very few taught us the proper way it should be done. There were a limited number of books on fasting available to me then.

Although there are many great books

on the subject today, and the Bible has so much to say on it, yet there is not much teaching in the church on this important doctrine. There is much more material available on fasting now, compared to thirty years ago; thank God for that. However, some of the books which have been written have not done justice to the subject. Particularly lacking is information on exactly what a fast is and how one should start and end a fast, especially a long, total fast, seven days and over.

When I broke my first seven days fast as a new Christian, it was with a ripe mango. Like I said before, I just did not know better. The mango was much too sour for my empty stomach at that time. It was like acid being poured into my stomach. I thought I would not survive. Thank God, after a few hours I got a relief. Maybe this is one of the reasons I began to study the subject more.

Fasting and praying is not something for God's people to be afraid of. We should be happy to engage in fasting. But because many do not have the true understanding of it, they are afraid to do what the Lord has commanded us to do.

Jesus made a statement that I find very interesting concerning the last days. In Matthew 24:37-39 he said,

"But as the days of Noe were, so shall also the coming of the Son of man be.

For as in the days that were before the flood, they were eating and drinking, marrying and giving in marriage, until the day that Noe entered the ark,

And knew not until the flood came, and took them all away; so shall also the coming of the Son of man be."

It seems that this scripture is being fulfilled among us. Now almost everywhere is a food spree. By the highways, by-ways, towns, villages, cities, inside and outside is food. Every occasion now is an opportunity for people to eat. There is always a food fair somewhere. It may not be called by that name, but be sure there will be lots of eating and drinking. It is like people cannot come together unless there will be food. Now you are probably thinking that I am talking about unbelievers only, but not at all. The eating spree is big in the church. The house of fasting has become the house of feasting. If a pastor calls for a time of fasting, no matter the urgency or need, whether it is on a Sunday or holiday, very few persons would turn out. The numbers are especially low if the fasting is more than two days. People tell themselves that they cannot stay so long without food.

We are not hearing from God because we are not spending adequate time with God. As the Apostle Paul says in Philippians 3:18-19,

"(For many walk, of whom I have told you often, and now tell you even weeping, that they are the enemies of the cross of Christ:

Whose end is destruction, whose God is their belly, and whose glory is in their shame, who mind earthly things.)"

Our god has become our belly. Whenever it says 'I need food' we give it food. We have no discipline over the food appetite. We need to crucify the food appetite at times. The last days are upon us. We have been carried away by food. This generation is a gluttonous generation, an obese generation that does not spend time in praying and fasting. The generation of the days of Noah is upon us. Is it time to seek the Lord, or time to eat and drink?

This book comes because I believe that God will allow it to be in the hands of the right people, who will take a stand to seek

His face in the deepest form of prayer there is, praying and fasting. In Matthew 4:4 Jesus said, *"It is written, Man shall not live by bread alone, but by every word that proceedeth out of the mouth of God."* And in Deuteronomy 8:3 we read,

"And he humbled thee, and suffered thee to hunger, and fed thee with manna, which thou knewest not, neither did thy fathers know; that he might make thee know that man doth not live by bread only, but by every word that proceedeth out of the mouth of the LORD doth man live."

There is a word that proceedeth out of the mouth of the Lord that says,

"Moreover when ye fast, be not, as the hypocrites, of a sad countenance: for they disfigure their faces, that they may appear unto men to fast. Verily I say unto you, They have their reward.

But thou, when thou fastest, anoint thine head, and wash thy face;

That thou appear not unto men to fast, but unto thy Father which is in secret: and thy Father, which seeth in secret, shall reward thee openly."

The word says 'when you fast' not 'if you fast'. God is expecting us to fast. In the same way He says 'when you pray' and 'when you give'; not 'if' but 'when'. Fasting must not be *if* but *when*.

God expects you to fast. We must make time to fast and seek His face. Fasting is an important teaching in both Old and New Testaments. Who fasted like Moses? Jesus, our supreme example, the Son of God fasted. The disciples of Jesus and the early church fasted and there were great results. Shall we not fast who are living in the last days? I believe now is the time to seek God in the greatest form of prayer that is available to man, and we shall see the glory of God if we do it right. This book is here to help you do it and do it right.

3
PRAYING AND FASTING DEFINED

Fasting is not just staying without food. There are many who are staying without food but that does not necessarily mean that they are praying to God. As a matter of fact, there are many staying without food, praying to the devil. There are those who are on hunger strikes for one reason or the other but they are not praying to God. On the other hand there are those who eat all day and say that they are fasting. They say that they are fasting from answering the phones or from using the computer, but not from food. I hear God saying, 'Do not make mockery with my word.' Will you call this a fast? Is this what God calls a fast?

Fasting is a means of humbling the soul before God. This is how David puts it in Psalm 35:13-14,

"But as for me, when they were sick, my clothing was sackcloth: I humbled my soul with fasting; and my prayer returned into mine own bosom.

I behaved myself as though he had been my friend or brother: I bowed down heavily, as one that mourneth for his mother."

It is a chastening of the soul. Psalm 69:10-15 reads,

"When I wept, and chastened my soul with fasting, that was to my reproach. I made sackcloth also my garment; and I became a proverb to them. They that sit in the gate speak against me; and I was the song of the drunkards. But as for me, my prayer is unto thee, O LORD, in an acceptable time: O God, in the multitude of

thy mercy hear me, in the truth of thy salvation. Deliver me out of the mire, and let me not sink: let me be delivered from them that hate me, and out of the deep waters. Let not the waterflood overflow me, neither let the deep swallow me up, and let not the pit shut her mouth upon me."

It is a time of crucifying the appetites and denying them so to give your entire time to deep prayer and meditation to God.

Fasting is a time of staying without food to seek God on specific matters, or great needs, or on things that are abnormal and need answers. For example, let us look at David in 2 Samuel 12:16-20.

"David therefore besought God for the child; and David fasted, and went in, and lay all night upon the earth.

And the elders of his house arose, and went to him, to raise him from the earth: but he would not, neither did he eat bread with them.

And it came to pass on the seventh day, that the child died. And the servants of David feared to tell him that the child was dead: for they said, Behold, while the child was yet alive, we spake unto him, and he would not hearken unto our voice: how will he then vex himself, if we tell him that the child is dead?

But when David saw that his servants whispered, David perceived that the child was dead: therefore David said unto his servants, Is the child dead? And they said, He is dead.

Then David arose from the earth, and washed, and anointed himself, and changed his apparel, and came into the house of the LORD, and worshipped: then he came to his own house; and when he required, they set bread before him, and he did eat."

4
DEVELOP FAITH AND CAST OUT DEVILS

The Bible records a situation where there was a child who was possessed with a dumb spirit. The child's father brought him to the disciples, but they could not cast him out. So when Jesus came, they brought the child to Him. After Jesus cast out the devil the disciples asked Him, *"Why could we not cast him out?"* In Matthew 17:20 He answered them and said,

"...it is because of your unbelief: for verily I say unto you, if ye have faith as a grain of mustard seed, ye shall say unto this mountain, Remove hence to yonder

place; and it shall remove; and nothing shall be impossible to you. Howbeit, this kind goeth not out but by prayer and fasting."

He said in some cases the only thing that will help is praying and fasting. Howbeit this kind goeth not out but by prayer and fasting. Some commentators question what Jesus meant by *"this kind."* Was it a demon? Is the text referring to unbelief or something else? No matter what, the unbelief was what prevented them from casting out the demon, or the particular type of demons. You can be certain that there are things we need to fast and pray about in order to get rid of them.

I must use one more biblical example because it is beautiful. It is a long portion, but you must read it. This portion of scripture relates when various armies came to fight against Judah. Judah decided that the only way out of the situation was if God helped them. So the leader, Jehoshaphat, called on all the people of Judah to seek the Lord in prayer and fasting. Let us look at what the Lord did in 2 Chronicles 20:1-25;

"And it came to pass after this also, that the children of Moab, and the children of Ammon, and with them other beside the Ammonites, came against Jehoshaphat to battle.

Then there came some that told Jehoshaphat, saying, There cometh a great multitude against thee from beyond the sea on this side Syria; and, behold, they be in Hazazontamar, which is Engedi.

And Jehoshaphat feared, and set himself to seek the LORD, and proclaimed a fast throughout all Judah.

And Judah gathered themselves together, to ask help of the LORD: even out of all the cities of Judah they came to seek the LORD.

And Jehoshaphat stood in the congregation of Judah and Jerusalem, in the house of the LORD, before the new court,

And said, O LORD God of our fathers, art not thou God in heaven? And rulest not thou over all the kingdoms of the heathen? And in thine hand is there not power and might, so that none is able to withstand thee?

Art not thou our God, who didst drive out the inhabitants of this land before thy people Israel, and gavest it to the seed of Abraham they friend for ever?

And they dwelt therein, and have built thee a sanctuary therein for thy name, saying,

If, when evil cometh upon us, as the sword, judgment, or pestilence, or famine, we stand before this house, and in thy presence, (for thy name is in this house,) and cry unto thee in our affliction, then thou wilt hear and help.

And now, behold, the children of Ammon and Moab and mount Seir, whom thou wouldest not let Israel invade, when they came out of the land of Egypt, but they turned from them, and destroyed them not;

Behold, I say, how they reward us, to come to cast out of thy possession, which thou hast given us to inherit.

O our God, wilt thou not judge them? For we have no might against this great company that cometh against us; neither know we what to do: but our eyes are upon thee.

And all Judah stood before the LORD, with their little ones, their wives, and their children.

Then upon Jahaziel the son Zechariah, the son of Benaiah, the son of Jeiel, the son of Mattaniah, a Levite of the sons of Asaph, came the Spirit of the LORD in the midst of the congregation;

And he said, Hearken ye, all Judah, and ye inhabitants of Jerusalem, and thou King Jehoshaphat, thus saith the LORD unto you, Be not afraid nor dismayed by reason of this great multitude; for the battle is not yours, but God's.

To morrow go ye down against them: behold, they come up by the cliff of Ziz; and ye shall find them at the end of the brook, before the wilderness of Jeruel.

Ye shall not need to fight in this battle: set yourselves, stand ye still, and see the salvation of the LORD with you, O Judah and Jerusalem: fear not, nor be dismayed; to morrow go out against them: for the LORD will be with you.

And Jehoshaphat bowed his head with his face to the ground: and all Judah and the inhabitants of Jerusalem fell before the LORD, worshipping the LORD.

And the Levites, of the children of the

Korhites, stood up to praise the LORD God of Israel with a loud voice on high.

And they rose early in the morning, and went forth into the wilderness of Tekoa: and as they went forth, Jehoshaphat stood and said, Hear me, O Judah, and ye inhabitants of Jerusalem; believe in the LORD your God, so shall ye be established; believe his prophets, so shall ye prosper.

And when he had consulted with the people, he appointed singers unto the LORD, and that should praise the beauty of holiness, as they went out before the army, and to say, Praise the LORD; for his mercy endureth for ever.

And when they began to sing and to praise, the LORD set ambushments against the children of Ammon, Moab, and mount Seir, which were come against Judah; and they were smitten.

For the children of Ammon and Moab stood up against the inhabitants of mount

Seir, utterly to destroy them: and when they had made an end of the inhabitants of Seir, every one helped to destroy another.

And when Judah came toward the watch tower in the wilderness, they looked unto the multitude, and, behold, they were dead bodies fallen to the earth, and none escaped.

And when Jehoshaphat and his people came to take away the spoil of them, they found among them in abundance both riches with the dead bodies, and precious jewels, which they stripped off for themselves, more than they could carry away: and they were three days in gathering of the spoil, it was so much."

The word says that the armies that came to fight against Judah began to fight among themselves. They killed each other, wiping out each other's armies. It would seem that they even wiped out their own armies. All the children of Israel had to do was collect the spoils. And the spoils were a great deal. When you walk right with the Lord, and you pray and fast, you won't have to do any physical fighting. God will do the fighting for you. He will take care of the enemy, no matter their numbers. Your biggest trouble would be to collect the spoils. No physical weapon from the children of Judah was used to win the battle; what was used was the mightiest weapon available to the children of God, the weapon of praying and fasting.

How devastating! The Lord sent ambushment against the children of Ammon, and Moab fought with the children of Mount Seir to slay and destroy them. And when they had made an end of the inhabitants of Seir, they fought among themselves to destroy each other. When we pray and fast, we put God's army to fight on our behalf and the benefit of that is we win the battle without even quarreling with the enemy; all we would have done was seek the face of God in prayer and fasting.

5
HOW IMPORTANT IS FASTING?

Many major events in history took place during a fast or right after a fast, or through a man or woman spending quality time praying and fasting. One of the greatest writings in history is the Ten Commandments. Several nations have based various parts of their laws on the Ten Commandments. As you know, this was the main law for the children of Israel. But how did Israel and the world receive this great instruction? It was the result of a man who prayed and fasted for forty days and forty nights; God gave him those great laws. He was not an angel, but a man like you and me. He had flaws like you and me. Yet, the Lord helped him fast without food for forty days and forty nights. By the way, Moses fasted for forty days, twice.

If God can help Moses, He can help you. I am not saying that you have to fast for forty days and forty nights. But, if the Lord wants you to, why not? Based on the scriptures we can deduce that Moses did not know how long he would have been there, but God sustained him. The children of Israel had not expected him to be there that long. As a matter of fact they started saying, "We don't know what is become of that Moses." As far as they were concerned Moses had been in the mountain for too long; it was time to move on.

The same attitude exists today. Some people have the notion that when you are spending time fasting you are wasting time. But time spent in the presence of God can never be wasted time. No matter how long God wants you to go, He will sustain you. And you must not allow the devil to distract you or tempt you to stop before your time. When you are in the presence of God like Moses was, you truly don't think about food. I must confess though, that I believe Moses' fast was a unique one, but not because of the forty days without food. I believe every man and woman of God who is healthy can fast for forty days and forty nights with water. But we see with Moses that he had neither food nor water. We will look at the importance of drinking water even when fasting. But Exodus 34:28 says,

"And he was there with the LORD forty days and forty nights; he did neither eat bread, nor drink water. And he wrote upon the tables the words of the covenant, the Ten Commandments."

Scripture records another very important event, maybe even more important that the giving of the law. I am referring to the beginning of the ministry of grace. The law came through Moses, but grace and truth came through Jesus Christ. God used a human being to introduce the law, one who had his own faults. But He used His only begotten Son to bring in grace, one who is sinless.

Jesus fasted and prayed for forty days and forty nights before He entered public ministry. Before He called the twelve apostles, before He turned water into wine, before He raised the dead, before He cast out devils, He first fasted and prayed for forty days and forty nights. It was right after fasting that he proclaimed in Luke 4:18-19,

"The Spirit of the Lord is upon me, because he hath anointed me to preach the gospel to the poor; he hath sent me to heal the brokenhearted, to preach deliverance to the captives and recovering of sight to the

blind, to set at liberty them that are bruised.

To preach the acceptable year of the Lord."

Here we see Jesus recognizing the importance of prayer and fasting. He did not do any mighty works before He first prayed and fasted for forty days and forty nights. Even the one who brought grace fasted for forty days. Therefore we can say that fasting played an important role under both covenants; both under the law and under grace.

The Bible records the story of Esther. We are told of Haman, a man of great honour, who wanted to wipe out the Jews. He had the position, popularity and the influence to carry out his plans. The book of Esther chapter three, records Haman's plan to have the Jews annihilated. In chapter 4:7-15, Mordecai, a Jew, Esther's uncle, told her of the plot that Haman had devised to destroy the Jews. When Queen Esther heard of the plot, she asked Mordecai to gather the Jews together and have them all praying and fasting for three days. They needed God to turn around the terrible massacre that Haman had intended against them. Esther herself promised to fast for three days without food and water and at the end of the fast she would go before the king in an effort to have him overturn the decision, even though it had been sealed with the king's ring.

After they had fasted for three days Esther went into the presence of the king, and gained favor with him. In the end the king overturned the plans of Haman who had plotted against the Jews, and he was hung in a place that he had prepared to hang Mordecai. Haman's entire household was killed as well and Mordecai was promoted to great honour by the king. All the Jews were saved because they had taken time to seek the face of God in prayer and fasting. They were preserved and their enemy was destroyed.

Fasting works. We see in Esther, an entire nation was spared because they prayed and fasted for three days. Maybe we can save a lot of our people if we spend time praying and fasting on their behalf. Maybe it will deliver our children and communities from the hands or plots of the enemy.

In the book of Acts we read the story of Cornelius. Let's read what he said in Acts 10:30-32.

"And Cornelius said, Four days ago I was fasting until this hour, and at the ninth hour I prayed in my house, and, behold, a man stood before me in bright clothing,

And said, Cornelius, thy prayer is heard, and thine alms are had in remembrance in the sight of God.

Send therefore to Joppa, and call hither Simon, whose surname is Peter; he is lodged in the house of one Simon a tanner by the sea side: who, when he cometh, shall speak with thee."

Here was a man who was not a Jew. He had not even been baptized. He was just a seeker of God. He was honest in his heart and prayed and fasted to God for direction, and God dispatched an angel to guide him. The angel gave him clear cut direction, what to do, where to go and who to ask for. When he followed the direction that came from heaven he found it just as the angel had declared. In spite of the Jewish tradition that dictated a Jew should not enter the house of a gentile, God had prepared Peter's heart to go to Cornelius's house. By the way, God showed Peter the same vision three times to prepare his heart before the messengers from Cornelius's house had arrived. When

Peter spoke to Cornelius and those who were at the house, they all got saved and were filled with the Holy Spirit, just as the hundred and twenty had been in the upper room in Acts chapter two.

One man's godly life, which included praying and fasting, broke a tradition that had existed for thousands of years. Peter went into a gentile house and ate with them and those who accompanied Peter were astonished as to what God was doing among the gentiles. People were converted, they spoke with other tongues, and they were baptized in water. I believe all that happened because of one man who was serious about praying and fasting.

I believe that fasting breaks yokes and sets people free. We read in the book of Acts 13:1-4;

"Now there were in the church that was at Antioch certain prophets and teachers; as Barnabas, and Simeon that was called

Niger, and Lucius of Cyrene, and Manaen, which had been brought up with Herod the tetrarch, and Saul.

As they ministered to the Lord, and fasted, the Holy Ghost said, Separate me Barnabas and Saul for the work whereunto I have called them.

And when they had fasted and prayed, and laid their hands on them, they sent them away.

So they, being sent forth by the Holy Ghost, departed unto Seleucia; and from thence they sailed to Cyprus."

Here we see the church of Christ praying and fasting and during that time they received ministerial guidance. The Holy Ghost said who among them that should go to the mission field. There are many people in our church today who don't know what ministry within the body they are called to. I am sure that if we seek God in prayer and fasting he will make it clear to us. This does not suggest that He cannot guide or call us outside of praying and fasting, but so many times in the scriptures we see him give guidance to His people after they pray and fast.

In the book of Daniel chapter 10, we have tremendous insight into the importance of praying and fasting. I don't want to take anything away from the text on this important subject, so let us allow the Bible to speak. Daniel 10:2-13;

"In those days I Daniel was mourning three full weeks.

I ate no pleasant bread, neither came flesh or wine in my mouth, neither did I anoint myself at all, till three whole weeks were fulfilled.

And in the four and twentieth day of the first month, as I was by the side of the great river, which is Hiddekel;

Then I lifted up mine eyes, and looked, and behold a certain man clothed in linen, whose loins were girded with fine gold of Uphaz:

His body also was like the beryl, and his face as the appearance of lightning, and his eyes as lamps of fire, and his arms and his feet like in colour to polished brass, and the voice of his words like the voice of a multitude.

And I Daniel alone saw the vision: for the men that were with me saw not the vision; but a great quaking fell upon them, so that they fled to hide themselves.

Therefore I was left alone, and saw this great vision, and there remained no strength in me: for my comeliness was turned in me into corruption, and I retained no strength.

Yet heard I the voice of his words: and when I heard the voice of his words, then was I in a deep sleep on my face, and my face toward the ground.

And, behold, an hand touched me,

which set me upon my knees and upon the palms of my hands.

And he said unto me, O Daniel, a man greatly beloved, understand the words that I speak unto thee, and stand upright: for unto thee am I now sent. And when he had spoken this word unto me, I stood trembling.

Then said he unto me, Fear not, Daniel: for from the first day that thou didst set thine heart to understand, and to chasten thyself before thy God, thy words were heard, and I am come for thy words.

But the prince of the kingdom of Persia withstood me one and twenty days: but, lo, Michael, one of the chief princes, came to help me; and I remained there with the kings of Persia."

I know that I have quoted quite a bit, but this portion is so good, that I did not know where to stop. By the way, I believe that you prefer to hear what the word of

God says on the subject, rather than just my opinion. So I am delighted to be able to share with you from the Bible. Let us see what light we get from this portion of scripture.

Daniel, one of God's servants went on a partial fast for twenty days. The text made it clear that it was a partial fast, for he said he was mourning three full weeks and he ate no pleasant bread, neither did flesh come to his mouth. It is possible that he took tea and juice.

The scripture reveals to us that because of this fast Daniel had an encounter with one of the angels of God. We also understand that Michael is one of the chief angels and has great power. He was able to set another angel free from the interception of a demonic spirit. In other words we understand through this text, and there are other supporting texts, that when we pray there are demonic spirits that hinder our prayers.

Maybe if Daniel had prayed for just one day he would not have received the answer. But because he persevered in prayer and fasting, God released another angel to ensure that his prayer was answered.

The text reveals a lot about spiritual warfare. There are different princes of demons over varying territories and they are fighting to maintain control over those areas. They are not letting go easily. We must fight to take control over our nations. If we pray, God will give us revelation but nothing contrary to the teaching of scripture; all revelations and prophecies should be tested by the word of God. There are some demons which are powerful. The angel said to Daniel, *"the prince of the kingdom of Persia withstood me one and twenty days"*, so it was a high ranking demon.

The Bible says that when the angel came there were others with Daniel. Maybe they had come to visit him, or perhaps they lived with him, we don't know for sure. What we do know is that they did not see the vision or the angel. The word says that a great quaking fell upon them, so they fled and hid themselves.

I believe that the people who will fast and pray will be a people of vision; God will show them things to come. God showed Daniel things that must come to pass while he was praying and fasting. There are some visions that not everyone can receive; some visions can only be handled by men and women who spend time praying and fasting.

6
THE FOOD PROBLEM

Some of the worst things that have happened in human history have happened because of a lack of discipline towards food. The first sin on earth came as a result of Satan tempting Eve to eat the forbidden fruit. Satan used food to deceive Eve. So the very first temptation recorded in the Bible had to do with food. Unfortunately, Satan got Eve to eat when she should not have eaten of that particular tree.

I believe that there are times that the Lord calls us into prayer and fasting but somehow we allow the devil to use food to deceive us, and so we are eating when we should be fasting. Or, we break the fast before time just because we are being tempted with food.

One of the reasons that God was greatly displeased with the children of Israel in the wilderness was their constant murmuring about food. They talked very little about the bondage they were under in Egypt and how many of their baby boys were killed. Their murmuring didn't cease even when God was feeding them supernaturally with manna from heaven which they did not even have to work for; it fell right at their tent doors. The point here is that we have to discipline ourselves when it comes to food. We must know when to put it aside and seek the face of God in fasting.

We see the Savior of the world, the one who came to die on the cross for the sins of mankind, after He had fasted for forty days and forty nights, the devil tried his best to kill Him by asking Him to turn stones into bread. If you eat bread after forty days of fasting you will die. There are times that the devil will use food to try to prevent us from fulfilling our purpose.

After Jesus' forty day fast, Satan used food as a temptation, just as he used food to tempt Eve.

So many have been sidetracked by food; they are unable to reach their destinies because they cannot discipline themselves when it comes to food. I believe that if people would pray and fast from time to time, they would live much healthier lives. This is what the Bible says about a fast that is done in the proper way;

"Then shall thy light break forth as the morning, and thine health shall spring forth speedily: and thy righteousness shall go before thee; the glory of the Lord shall be thy rereward."

Thomas Eristhee

7
THE DOCTRINE OF PRAYER AND FASTING

This doctrine is not a verse here, and a random verse there which are taken out of context. There are large portions of passages that address the subject of prayer and fasting. Some chapters within scripture focus on the matter of praying and fasting. One such example is Isaiah 58; another is Daniel chapters 9 and 10, and there are many others. For God to devote so much time in the Bible to prayer and fasting means it must be an important subject.

In the scriptures the word 'fasting' is used more than many other major doctrines. It is used in both Old and New

Testaments. The words fast, fasted, fastest, fasting and fastings are used more than a hundred times in the Bible. If a word is used so many times, it must be of much importance. Additionally, the word 'fast' is used in about half of the 66 books of the Bible. The majority of the writers in the Bible used the word, as well as major figures in the Bible, such as Christ, the Pharisees, John the Baptist and many others.

8
THE BENEFITS OF FASTING

Maybe the best place to begin talking about the benefits of fasting is to go to the word of God in Isaiah 58:6-12. There are a lot of benefits mentioned in that portion of scripture.

"Is this not the fast that I have chosen? To loose the bands of wickedness, to undo the heavy burdens, and to let the oppressed go free, and that ye break every yoke?

Is it not to deal thy bread to the hungry, and thou bring the poor that are cast out to thy house? When thou seest the naked, that thou cover him; and that thou hide not thyself from thine own flesh?

Then shall thy light break forth as the morning, and thine health shall spring forth speedily: and thy righteousness shall go before thee; the glory of the LORD shall be thy rereward.

Then shalt thou call, and the LORD shall answer; thou shalt cry, and he shall say, Here I am. If thou take away from the midst of thee the yoke, the putting forth of the finger, and speaking vanity;

And if thou draw out thy soul to the hungry, and satisfy the afflicted soul: then shall thy light rise in obscurity, and thy darkness be as the noonday:

And the LORD shall guide thee continually, and satisfy thy soul in drought, and make fat thy bones: and thou shalt be like a watered garden, and like a spring of water, whose waters fail not.

And they that shall be of thee shall build the old waste places: thou shalt raise up the foundations of many generations;

and thou shalt be called, The repairer of the breach, The restorer of paths to dwell in."

'Is not this the fast that I have chosen? To loose the bands of wickedness, to undo the heavy burdens and to let the oppressed go free, and that thou break every yoke?'

These are rhetorical questions. The verses before had been talking about the wrong reasons for fasting. Now the writer gives the right reasons to fast and he is saying that if we do it the right way there are many benefits to be gained from fasting. Those benefits extend to other persons and nations as well.

Isaiah goes on to say through our fasting we should seek God to loose the bands of wickedness, injustice, lawlessness, to undo everything that has been tied unjustly against someone. Fasting will loose the yoke that has been over the necks of the people. It will let the oppressed go free. Remember, it is a time that we spend before God, asking Him to help us against ungodliness. We desire to see those who have been oppressed by their fellowman and by the devil walk in freedom. Fasting will break yokes of slavery, poverty, unbelief, and spiritual blindness; it will set people free from curses and remove burdens from their shoulders.

Fasting will cause us to be more compassionate. The word says that we bring the poor that are cast out into our houses. That means the homeless. In other words, if we fast properly, we will be more concerned about the things that God is concerned about. If it was not for the mercies of God we all would have been homeless, but the Lord reached down and helped us so that we can reach out and help others. It is not easy to do that but fasting makes it easier and God gives direction and the ability to do it.

Fasting will cause us to have a better view of mankind and how we can help others. The scripture quoted earlier says that if you fast properly then your light will break forth as the morning, and your health shall spring forth speedily, and your righteousness shall go before you, and the glory of the Lord will be your rereward. You are going to have light as the morning; you will not walk in darkness; you will be a person of vision; you will know where to go, what to do and how to do it. God gave Daniel clear cut vision and understanding about His kingdom and His children through prayer and fasting. One of the many blessings of praying and fasting is the victory of receiving light and direction from the Lord; when we fast we receive answers from God on matters we are not clear about.

The text says that your health will

spring forth speedily. Praying and fasting the right way may bring quick healings. We may never know how many surgeries or diseases we have avoided because we have been praying and fasting. Your righteousness will go before you and God will exalt you because you did not fast to be seen of man; you did not fast as a hypocrite. You fasted with the right motive; God will cause His righteousness to go before you, He will give you favour and bless you the right way because you fasted the right way.

God will allow man to testify of your goodness. The glory of the Lord will be your rereward. The presence of God will be with you like it was with the children of Israel in the wilderness, and as it was at the dedication of Solomon's temple. One of the saddest commentaries in the Old Testament speaks of when the glory of God departed from the children of Israel.

Without the glory of God we are defeated. There is nothing better than having the glory of God as your reward. Moses said, "*Lord if thy presence go not with me, carry us not up hence*" Exodus 33:15. What makes the difference is the glory of God. The glory of God was with Moses when he came down from the mountain, from the presence of God. The Bible says that he had to cover his face with a veil. You may not always see the glory, but the demons see the glory. Do you remember what the evil spirit said to the sons of Sceva in Acts 19:15? *'Paul I know, Jesus I know, but who are you?'* No glory. The devil cannot touch the life with the glory of God on it.

There are times when we pray, and it looks as if our prayers are not reaching the throne of God, our answers seem delayed or it seems like we are not hearing from God. Maybe that is the moment to take some time out with God in prayer and fasting. Look at your life. Ask yourself, 'What might be hindering me? Am I too busy with the affairs of this life? Is my spiritual life suffering because of that? Am I going in the wrong direction?' When you come to God with an honest heart He will help you, He will show you your errors and He will unclog the channels that are not receiving the signals. The word says in Isaiah 58:9,

"Then shalt thou call, and the LORD shall answer; thou shalt cry, and he shall say, Here I am. If thou take away from the midst of thee the yoke, the putting forth of the finger, and speaking vanity".

When we put our house together God will hear us; praying and fasting is one means of putting it together. When we have done that the words says, then shall we call and He will answer, He will say 'Here I am'. He will not seem distant, but a very present help, 'Here I am'. He is not just in heaven, but very close to you, with you; His voice can be heard right now, 'Here I am'.

There is nothing as special as being acquainted with hearing the voice of God and hearing it often. It is one of the greatest treasures of God's people. Conversely, if you have been accustomed to hearing His voice, there is nothing as miserable as not being able to hear it anymore. Hearing the voice of God is one of the greatest blessings of the Christian life. When we reach the place where we no longer hear the voice of God, it may be the result of sin in our lives, or perhaps continuous disobedience to something that the Holy Spirit is asking us to do and we refuse to do it. You see, these things are possible. Jesus says if we don't forgive others, neither will our Father in heaven forgive us. Now if He does not forgive us how can He hear us? Unforgiveness can prevent us from hearing God. Jesus says if you come to the altar with your gift and you remember that your brother has trespassed against you, go and make it right with him and then come and offer your gift.

These things prevent us from hearing the voice of God. When we do not hear from God, life becomes frustrating. You who have been acquainted with His voice but not hearing it anymore, become like a fish out of water. You are in a place you don't belong. But when you are hearing the voice of God there is a fresh fire in your heart; it does not matter what people say or do, something pushes you forward in the Lord.

Hearing the voice of God could cause a man to change a nation. My friends, the voice of God is powerful, yet to His children, it is so gentle and refreshing, so inspiring. Just hearing one word from God can change the course of your life.

Spending time in praying and fasting prepares your heart to hear the voice of the Lord. It unclogs the channels that may have been closed, that prevented you from hearing God as you ought, and it gives you a fresh start. He will say 'Here I am'. Your light shall arise in darkness. Even in darkness God will make a way for the man who knows how to seek Him in prayer and fasting. He will turn calamity to triumph, He will give you good success, and your adversity shall be turned to prosperity, your darkness to light, weeping to joy. He will turn your mourning to dancing. The Lord will guide you continually. Now tell me who does not want such a blessing.

The word of God says it is possible for Him to guide you continually if you will seek Him in prayer and fasting; God will be your continuous guide. What a blessing, what security, to have God as our constant guide in this world. Yes, there are traps along the way that we know nothing about; thank God that He is all-knowing and all-seeing and He is with us to guide us continually.

Saint Lucia has a lot of beautiful scenery; magnificent mountain peaks, valleys, sulphur springs and rain forests, among other things. But to enjoy them you need a guide who knows the place to lead you. There can be great dangers for a visitor who attempts to climb the mountains without a guide. One can even die in the process, or get lost. Do you know how many persons have died trying to climb Mount Everest even with a guide? You see, on this earth we are visitors, we are strangers and pilgrims. We don't know the way, and I tell you there are dangers all around us, some we can see, and many we cannot see; some physical and others spiritual. So we need a guide but a human guide is incapable of such a task. We need spiritual guidance. The word of the Lord says if we pray and fast properly the Lord Himself will guide us continually, not for one day, but continually.

My friends, we have a guide, but not just any guide; God Himself. What a blessing. This world is filled with spiritual traps. It is a great wilderness of evil and we don't understand everything about the enemy. He is an old serpent filled with tricks, but with God as our continuous guide we will make it to the Promised Land. There were times that the children of Israel did not even see a way; there was no way, but because God was with them He created a way through the Red Sea. His children passed through on dry ground. The enemy attempted but could not pass. The same path became a grave, their final resting place, because God was not their guide. What a guide we have! When there is no way He will make a way for those who will pray and fast.

Could you imagine the sights that you will see as God guides you in prayer and fasting? What levels He will take you to! Could you imagine the fellowship that you will have with Him as you work following the Divine leader? David was a man who prayed and fasted much. In Psalm 23:4 he said, *"Yea, though I walk through the valley of the shadow of death, I will fear no evil: for thou art with me; thy rod and thy staff they comfort me."* David could have said so because he had God as his constant guide. When God is with you, you can go through the valleys, up the mountains and through the floods, because the guide is with you. Such are the benefits for the people of God who are willing to obey His teaching.

We are not saved by works, but Jesus says *'you are my disciples indeed if you do the things that I have commanded you'*, and God expects His children to take time out with Him in fasting. In our Christian life there are sacrifices that we have to make in order to see changes we desire. If we want souls to be saved, we must witness to them, tell them about God. If we want to receive we must give. In the same way, there are benefits that will accompany praying and fasting. The word is very clear on that matter.

Now you would have thought that we have discussed some serious benefits for far, but there is so much more to receive for the one who will make up his mind to get into the greatest form of prayer there is which is fasting, the absence of food. So many more benefits await the person who is determined to seek the face of God Almighty in times of great need. You have to pray that His will be done in your life, in that of your family, church and nation.

I pray that God will get more of His people saying "Here I am Lord; I make myself available."

God has promised to satisfy you in drought if you will seek His face in prayer and fasting. There is an account in the book of 1 Kings 17:1-6, about a drought that was on the land of Israel which lasted for three years. People were dying; it was a terrible famine. During that famine God took care of His servant Elijah, a man who we know spent quality time in fasting with God. As a matter of fact the Bible named him as one of the few in scripture that fasted for forty days and forty nights. This is found in 1 Kings 19:7-8.

"And the angel of the LORD came again the second time and touched him, and said, Arise and eat; because the journey is too great for thee.

And he arose, and did eat and drink, and went in the strength of that meat forty days and forty nights unto Horeb the mount of God."

The point is that God will take care of those who seek Him in fasting even during a famine. And I used Elijah as one of those we know who fasted and we know how the Lord took care of him in the midst of the famine. God caused ravens to bring him bread and flesh in the morning and bread and flesh in the evening. He allowed the brook to have water to sustain Elijah for a period of time. When you are a child of God who seeks him in sincerity, in fasting, His word says in Isaiah 58:11,

"And the LORD shall guide thee continually, and satisfy thy soul in drought, and make fat thy bones: and thou shalt be like a watered garden, and like a spring of water, whose waters fail not."

He will sustain you in times of drought. He sustained Elijah; He will sustain you as well. He sustained him by using the most unlikely animal, a raven, to carry food to him. These birds will consume all they can get, but the Lord changed their natural instincts and their first reaction was to bring food to Elijah during a time of famine.

The man who humbles himself before God in prayer and fasting will be sustained by God, even in times of famine. The story of God sustaining Elijah during a drought is quite a story. After He used the unlikely source of a raven, after the brook dried up, He used another unlikely source; He used a widow. God has more than a million ways to take care of us. You see a lot of times people make excuses for not praying and fasting; one of the excuses is "Who will provide for me if I take a week off from my job to seek the face of God in prayer and fasting?" Listen, God is asking you to take time out with Him in fasting. He will take care of the bills and other needs. He will make a way. He already knows what He will do. All you need to do is obey Him. He will take care of you even during a famine. This is a blessing for those who will pray and fast the right way.

I read about a young man by the name of Christmas Evans who many times spent morning till evening praying without food, just seeking God. He was mightily used by God to bring revival. John Welsh, another minister of the gospel, would sometimes spend eight to ten hours with God before he could eat.

I am not saying that the only people God will provide for in famine are those who fast for the right reason. No, not at all. God has promised in His word to be faithful to those who are faithful to Him. What I am saying is that He promised that those who will fast the right way will definitely receive that promised blessing or benefit, but it does not mean that it belongs to them exclusively. He will make your bones fat. What does that mean? It means that the Lord will prosper you. Some see it as your strength being renewed. As the prophet said in Isaiah 40:30-31,

"Even the youths shall faint and be weary, and the young men shall utterly fall: But they that wait upon the LORD shall renew their strength; they shall mount up with wings as eagles; they shall run, and not be weary; and they shall walk, and not faint."

Fasting is one way of waiting on the Lord. You will be like a watered garden. The first Psalm tells us that a man that is like a tree planted by the rivers of water shall always bear fruit in his season. He leaf shall not wither and whatsoever he doeth shall prosper. So the man who prays and fasts is like a watered garden.

He is always green; there is nothing like drought for him. The dryness may be happening around him but he remains watered by the Lord.

I am trying to say that it pays to fast. God has promised a lot of blessings on the person who seeks Him in prayer and fasting, who does not seek Him just because of the benefits; but there are fringe benefits that He adds. It is like God putting a drip irrigation system around you. You are always getting water. Therefore you are always bearing fruits. What does the farmer want more than fruit? What does God want from us but fruits? Jesus cursed the fig tree because it had no fruit. The Father desires that we bear much fruit. A man, a woman who seeks God in prayer and fasting, will receive fertilizer so that fruits can be produced. Yes, that man who prays and fasts will attract the world with his fruits;

everybody loves to see a tree that is full of fruit. And that refers to both the saved and unsaved; Jesus said that the world will know us by our fruits.

Fasting causes us to bear fruits because it allows us to look at ourselves, to look at what is hindering the flow of the Holy Spirit in our lives. It has a way of exposing the big sins as well as the little ones, even the weight that so easily besets us. Fasting helps us to destroy the bad habits that keep us bound, and slay the flesh. It is like servicing the body. Just as one services a vehicle after a specific number of miles, so we too, need to take time and wait on God; we need to allow Him to service us for better use in His kingdom and against the kingdom of darkness. They that wait upon the Lord shall renew their strength.

The one who fasts will be like a spring of water that does not fail. Water is very essential to life. We cannot last long without water, but we can live longer without food. I will talk about this a little later. We live in a world where people are thirsty not for physical water but spiritual drink, spiritual satisfaction. God wants to use us a pipeline to bring this spiritual supply to a world that is drying. We must constantly stay connected to the spring of living water, so that our water never runs dry. We have to minister from the abundance that is flowing out of us. 'Out of your bellies', Jesus says, 'shall flow rivers of living water.'

There are many springs that are dry in the summertime. They only have water during the rainy season, when there is water everywhere else. But for the man or the woman who spends time praying and fasting, God says that individual shall be like a spring of water that does not fail. It is not dependant on the season. He never has a dry season because God is his source. There are times when the taps are dry and the rivers have no water. Many countries have experienced crop failure because of lack of rain. Due to lack of water people are dying. But thank God for those who seek His face in prayer and fasting; they will prevent crop failure.

The one who prays and fasts properly will see his people, his generation, rebuilding the old waste places. There are a lot of holy things that have been broken down and need to be rebuilt; integrity in the church, faith, holiness, the fear of the Lord, deliverance for the captives, the possessed need to be free, there is a need for restoration of proper family life, and we can go on and on. It is like the days of Nehemiah. The walls are broken down, the church has no more strength, and the enemy has taken many captive. Somebody needs to rebuild the wall. We need to do like Nehemiah did when he heard of the condition of Jerusalem, how it was destroyed and wasted. He made up his mind to rebuild the city, to restore the broken places. But even before he attempted any restoration or rebuilding, let us look at what he did first in Nehemiah 1:4-6;

"And it came to pass, when I heard these words, that I sat down and wept, and mourned certain days, and fasted, and prayed before the God of heaven,

And said, I beseech thee, O LORD God of heaven, the great and terrible God, that keepeth covenant and mercy for them that love him and observe his commandments:

Let thine ear now be attentive, and thine eyes open, that thou mayest hear the prayer of thy servant, which I pray before thee now, day and night for the children of Israel thy servants, and confess the sins of the children of Israel, which we have sinned against thee: both I and my father's house have sinned."

Here we see among the first things that Nehemiah did when he heard of the condition of his country was fast and pray. Thank God He heard his prayer and helped him and restored the broken places, despite the fears of the opposition. Yes, God has promised that if we seek Him in prayer and fasting, He will use us to restore the old waste places. Isaiah 58:12 says,

"And they that shall be of thee shall build the old waste places: thou shalt raise up the foundations of many generations; and thou shalt be called, The repairer of the breach, The restorer of paths to dwell in."

Our fasting will not just be beneficial to us and to our families; it will affect generations that are not yet even born, it will change the environment and the attitude of nations. It will bring a sense of the fear of God in the land. It will rebuild the principles of God which have been broken down. It will bring changes in the laws of the government. It will bring back the fear of God in the church again. It will repair broken family altars. It will bring back effective evangelism. There will be genuine repentance in the church. There will be powerful messages in the pulpit. God is looking for men who will stand in the gap and pray and fast for restoration in the church and nation.

Thomas Eristhee

9
WHEN SHOULD I FAST

There are various times and seasons in our lives when we should fast. Before going to the biblical reasons which are many, maybe I should give a personal thought on that. Whenever I begin to feel dry, not hearing from God as I should be, I know it is time for me to seek God in prayer and fasting. When it seems that the Spirit of God is not moving in the church as He should be, worship seems dead, there is no zeal for evangelism, immorality is creeping in among members, discouragement is on every side, it is time to seek the Lord. When people of God have no desire to come to church, when people are not attending prayer meetings and bible study, it is time to seek the Lord. When the family life of the people of God is like that of the world, or in some cases worse, it is time to seek the Lord. When corruption is in the church as well as the government, it is time to seek the Lord. When the gospel is being preached just to make money, it is time to seek the Lord in serious praying and fasting. When crime and violence is increasing in the land and the justice system seems to be corrupt or unable to deliver justice, it is time to seek the Lord. When the righteous are being killed or persecuted, when innocent blood is being shed, when starvation is all around us and families are being displaced, it is time to pray and fast.

I believe that the power of prayer and fasting is the greatest power there is and we must use it. I also believe that God impresses upon His people times when they should seek His face in fasting. Here is what the prophet Joel says in Joel 2:15-18;

"Blow the trumpet in Zion, sanctify a fast, call a solemn assembly:

Gather the people, sanctify the congregation, assemble the elders, gather the children, and those that suck the breasts: let the bridegroom go forth of his chamber, and the bride out of her closet.

Let the priests, the ministers of the LORD, weep between the porch and the altar, and let them say, Spare thy people, O LORD, and give not thine heritage to reproach, that the heathen should rule over them: wherefore should they say among the people, Where is their God?

Then will the LORD be jealous for his land, and pity his people."

So there are times that God will impress the leaders to call the congregation, to call the people to a fast. But God expects us as individuals to take time regularly to pray and fast. He has already told us in His word that we have to pray and fast. He said in Matthew 6:16-18,

"Moreover when ye fast, be not, as the hypocrites, of a sad countenance: for they disfigure their faces, that they may appear unto men to fast. Verily I say unto you, They have their reward.

But thou, when thou fastest, anoint thine head, and wash thy face; that thou appear not unto men to fast, but unto thy Father which is in secret: and thy Father, which seeth in secret, shall reward the openly."

Not *if* you fast, *when* you fast. Fasting is something God expects His people to do. He expects it just as He expects them to give and to pray. There will always be reasons to fast; we cannot justify not fasting by saying that we will not fast unless God asks us to. We don't do that when we give or when we pray. Situations move us to pray and to give. The same should move us to fast.

When the people of Nineveh were told that their sins were great before God and that He would destroy the city, they took deliberate action. The prophet didn't have to tell them to fast. They decided that if they turned from their sins and sought God in prayer and fasting He may spare them. So they fasted for three days; from the greatest among them to the smallest. And God repented of the evil that He had determined to do to them.

Esther heard of the evil that was determined by Haman against the Jews and she and her people prayed and fasted and God delivered them. Conditions pushed them to seek God for help in prayer and fasting. It was not God coming to them saying, 'you must fast now', like He did to Moses when He called him up the mountain for forty days and forty nights. No, they saw the need to take serious time before God on particular matters.

Daniel needed answers from God; it took him twenty one days in prayer and fasting before he could get them. I believe that just as Nineveh saw a mighty revival, if we as a church would seek God in prayer and fasting with all our hearts, we too will see a revival in this sinful generation. There are more than one hundred reasons why we should pray and fast. If things were bad before the first coming of Christ to earth, I believe it will get much worse before His return for the church. Let us pray and fast for a harvest before it is too late.

There are some in the church today who are hoping for the return of the good old days; the days when we saw healings, miracles and great conviction of the Holy

Spirit upon unbelievers. Some of them came to the church sometimes to disturb, but God convicted them of their sins and they confessed publicly and repented. There was such great unity of God's people. Churches were built without money, because the churches were poor. But people turned out to work in great numbers and gave whatever little they had.

Many of us long to see those days again, but we forget that in those days the people of God spent much time in prayer and fasting. On many Sundays and holidays people would stay in church seeking God's face. Not today though. We plan for every holiday on the calendar to do something that is not church related and we neglect the time to pray and fast. Yet we say we want the good old days. But we cannot have the good old days without the good old habits.

10
OVERCOMING TEMPTATION IN PRAYING AND FASTING

Even while you are praying and fasting you will be severely tempted by the devil. As a matter of fact many people have started fasts and because of the severity of the temptation they ended the fast prematurely. Many don't realize that it was the devil that caused them to break the fast. They did not recognize it as a temptation of the devil because Satan is so skillful in tempting us. But there is great anointing to be received when you have overcome temptation and end your fast properly.

We want to look at Jesus' forty days of

fasting, but before we do that we want to look at the man who baptized Him and introduced Him to the world. I am talking about John the Baptist. The word says, concerning him, that his food was locust and wild honey. In Matthew 11:18 Jesus said of him, *"For John came neither eating nor drinking, and they say, He hath a devil."*

I understand that to mean that food appetite did not have the mastery over him. In our day food seems to control us instead of us determining what and when we will eat. So we hear what Jesus says about John concerning food. Let's see what John's own disciples said about him as it pertained to food and the kind of life he lived. Matthew 9:14, *"Then came to him the disciples of John, saying, why do we and the Pharisees fast oft, but thy disciples fast not?"* This says that John and his disciples used to fast often. The Pharisees fasted often as well, but we will not make much of the Pharisees because their motives were wrong; they did it just to be seen of men. Therefore they could not be heard by God; they received the praise of men as their reward. Let us read Jesus' response to the question of the disciples; Matthew 9:15,

"And Jesus said unto them, Can the children of the bridechamber mourn, as long as the bridegroom is with them? But the days will come, when the bridegroom shall be taken from them, and then shall they fast."

Jesus did not rebuke them for asking Him why the disciples were not fasting, but told them because He is with them now they don't need to fast; but when He shall be taken away from them, then they shall fast. So now is the time for us to fast, because Jesus is not with us physically; He has been taken away; it is time to mourn. Because we still have to do the works that He did and even greater, we need great anointing and one of the ways to receive it is through prayer and fasting.

Let us now turn our attention to the fasting of Jesus and the temptation of Satan. The devil tried his best to prevent Jesus from fulfilling His ministry on earth even before He began. But Jesus resisted him and moved into ministry with the anointing of the Holy Spirit upon His life. Mark 1:12-13 says,

"And immediately the Spirit driveth him into the wilderness. And he was there in the wilderness forty days, tempted of Satan; and was with the wild beasts; and angels ministered unto him."

Here we see Jesus' dependency on the Holy Spirit; He was fully God and fully man. He was totally dependent on the Holy Spirit while He was here on earth. This is how we are supposed to function here as well, being fully led by the Holy Spirit. The Holy Spirit drove Him to the wilderness to fast and to overcome the temptation of the devil.

The church has left fasting for feasting, yet we want the anointing of the Holy Spirit. When you are fasting you will be tempted of the devil but the Spirit will help you if you rely on Him.

At the time of fasting you must make sure that you put everything in place at home before you begin to fast. If the enemy can get any space in the family, he will accuse you. So you must make certain that you make adequate preparation for the family. And your family has to understand that you must take this time out with the Lord. You must cover your family in prayer while you are fasting because if the enemy can, he will try his best for something to go wrong with them, to try to get to you. If you are a pastor or a leader in the church, you must cover the church because if the enemy can, he will cause trouble, especially if you are on a long fast. I believe that if it is a long fast, not with the church, that the pastor or leader should take time away from the church. And I call anything from twenty days and over, long. Go to a place where you will not be disturbed; so that you can talk with God without being interrupted by the daily activities. This is important because you may find yourself so involved that you spend the day without food and without prayer. So, although you are not eating, you are not spending time with the Lord either.

Fasting requires great discipline; you must discipline your flesh and your mind. The devil truly attacks the mind in times of fasting, but you must let the Spirit of God have total control. The Bible says that Jesus was there with the wild beasts.

When you are fasting by yourself for a long time it can be very lonely, especially if it is a long fast.

At times after such a fast, you begin to get greater revelation than you were getting during the fast, therefore even after the fast you must be careful how you live; you should maintain a great attitude of prayer and worship. At the end of Jesus' fasting we saw the beauty of fasting. That is true also for most fasts recorded in the scriptures. We read in Matthew 4:11 that at the end of Jesus' fasting angels came and ministered unto Him. Moses' face shone so brilliantly that he had to put a veil over it. In the case of Nineveh, the entire city was saved after three days of fasting. Daniel had angels come and minister to him. Angels appeared to Cornelius and gave him clear cut directions as to what to do. Tell me how else we can have angels to visit us. Can we pay God some money? No. he wants to see a broken and a contrite spirit; that, he will not despise. Did He not say blessed are the poor in spirit for theirs is the kingdom of heaven? He said blessed are they that mourn for they shall be comforted. The poor in spirit realize that they cannot make it by themselves, that they need God's spirit. They need God's help and His strength. They may look weak on the outside but God has given them strength on the inside.

They mourn because they cannot do it without God. We want to be comforted by the comforter, but we don't want to mourn for Him. Many of us don't sense Him, yet we are not bothered. We don't hear Him for days, yet we will not mourn. We need men and women in the church who will mourn because of the condition of the church. There is no mourning in the church, yet we seem to have church. We want to see angels; we want to have great preaching and miraculous healings without the power of the Holy Spirit upon our lives. They that mourn shall be comforted. After Jesus had fasted for forty days and forty nights the Bible says He returned in the power of the Spirit. The word reads in Luke 4:18,

"The Spirit of the Lord is upon me, because he hath anointed me to preach the gospel to the poor; he hath sent me to heal the brokenhearted, to preach deliverance to the captives, and recovering of sight to the blind, to set at liberty them that are bruised,

To preach the acceptable year of the Lord."

He was able to say that after he had prayed and fasted forty days and forty nights. He came in the power of the Spirit.

As He walked, there was such an anointing upon His life; not just as he taught, preached or prayed, but as He walked. He walked by the Sea of Galilee, among fishermen, but the anointing was very strong upon Him; it had compelling power on those He called, no matter how bad they were. He called Andrew and his brother. They were casting their nets into the sea; they were busy working hard, but the anointing that was upon Jesus' life attracted them and they left everything and followed Him. The Bible states that they left everything and followed Him. That means they did not think about it, they just followed Him. They did not think about family, they did not think about what they would eat, they just followed Him. Their nets must have cost them much money, but they left them and followed Jesus. The anointing upon His life could not be resisted, it attracted them.

The anointing will give authority. The

Bible says concerning Jesus that He preached as one who had authority and not as a scribe. The scribes knew the scriptures but they did not have the power of the scripture. This is like so many of us today. We know the scripture but there is no power. We give much time to study but little time to pray and fast. Therefore we have little power.

The church needs to amaze the world again. Many are possessed and seemingly they cannot find deliverance. Oh that God will raise men and women who will pray and fast; believers who will work with such an anointing of God upon their lives that demons will cry out and the people will be delivered. May God raise you up!

Thomas Eristhee

11
FASTING HELPS GET THE JOB DONE

After Jesus had prayed and fasted for forty days and forty nights, the Bible says in Mark 1:33-34,

"And all the city was gathered together at the door. And he healed many that were sick of divers diseases, and cast out many devils; and suffered not the devils to speak, because they knew him."

The city was gathered to hear him. The anointing on His life drew the people to Him and He was able to meet all their needs. He healed the sick and cast out devils. That began to happen after He had prayed and fasted for forty days and forty nights. The people came from every quarter to hear Him. The greatest need of the church is not money as some seem to think. I believe the problem is the lack of the presence of God in the church, lack of power to meet the needs of this present day.

People have real problems; problems that only the church should be equipped to handle, because they are of a spiritual nature. There are problems of demon possession, evil spirits in people, curses and so on. You see, the other professions are not able to deal with those matters, because as I said, these are spiritual matters. But when the church, who is supposed to deal with it cannot, because we have not taken time to be in the presence of God for Him to equip us to meet those needs, then people are left hopeless.

Now, this is not the will of God. He has

said 'go heal the sick, cleanse the leper, cast out devils.' But there are some that will not be cast out except we spend time in prayer and fasting. Jesus said in Matthew 17:21, *"this kind goeth not out but by prayer and fasting."* So fasting helps us to reach the multitude that are possessed and have none to deliver them.

The church is becoming like the Pharisees' church; we say we believe in miracles, healings, angels and all the supernatural, but we are not seeing any of it happening in the church. Yet, we are not asking why. And I am saying that one of the reasons it is not happening as it should be, is that we are not spending enough time in the presence of God. We have not allowed Him to deal with us as individuals and also to anoint us for the work of the ministry.

The devil will tempt you to not fast. He will try all in his power to prevent you from fasting. And if you are able to resist and you begin the fast, then he starts to tempt you to break it before time. There must be something good about fasting, because the devil tries so hard to prevent you from doing it. He knows it helps you defeat his kingdom. Through fasting you don't just get victory over demons, but you get victory over the flesh, over strongholds in your life. You see, during fasting, God will show you the things in your life that are wrong, things that you need to get rid of.

When you are fasting the devil will use all forms of temptation that he can use. He will tempt you with sex, he will tempt you with loneliness, he will tempt you with food in the midst of your fasting; you will dream about food. You may even think that God is giving you the signal that you should stop the fast. We must resist him and the flesh, and follow the leading of the

Spirit of God. He will accuse you of wasting time; he will try to make you believe you have prayed long enough, that God has heard your prayers. But we should not take orders from the devil. We need to resist him!

There are times in your fasting that the enemy will try to make things go wrong at home just to try to cause you to stop your fast before time. There is a real battle going on at the time of fasting as the book of Daniel indicates; it speaks of the war that was between the angel of the Lord and the evil spirit that did not want Daniel to receive the message from God. Friends, praying and fasting is serious warfare. There is no greater form of prayer and the devil will do all in his power to try to hinder you from doing it. But we must be crucified that Christ might live in us and one way to do that is through prayer and fasting.

When Moses saw the children of Israel worshipping the golden calf, he went back to the mountain to pray and fast for another forty days and forty nights. Sin has a way of driving the true child of God back to the presence of God not just because of his own sins but also because of the sins of others.

In Exodus 32, God told Moses, *"...let me alone, that my wrath may wax hot against them, and that I may consume them: and I will make of thee a great nation."* But Moses said no. He stood before God on behalf of the people and God changed His mind, because of one man who fasted and prayed for forty. It was not easy for Moses. Remember he had just fasted for forty days before that, and he had to return a second time. But at times, to save lives, there must be great sacrifice. At times it may be that you have to leave your comfortable home, your job, at times your family, for the mission field. But there are lives that have to be saved and God may be calling you to make the sacrifice. Again, there are times that we have to make sacrifices in order to save lives.

Thomas Eristhee

12
STARTING THE FAST

There are things we need to know about beginning a fast, especially if you don't have much experience in fasting. You should start preparing your body for the fast. It is not time to stuff your body with food; you should not do that just before or right after a fast. The more you fill your stomach, the more work you are giving it to do, therefore when you wake up in the morning, you are hungry. So you should take something light the night before your fast.

If it is your first fast, don't fast for ten days, except you know for sure that is what God wants you to do. I would advise that you do between one and three days for your first fast. Now remember you have not gone this way before, so your body will react to the changes. Your stomach will tell your mind that you have not taken anything for the day, so you may feel hungry a little, but remember you are fasting. You will not die, neither will you cause any harm to your body if you fast a day, using only water.

I heard a story of two Christian brothers from a church I used to pastor. The incident happened before I became the pastor there. They were getting ready for a week of fasting. On their way to the venue where the fasting was to take place, they decided to have a last meal. One of the brothers had fifty cents, and the other had no money. The one with the money purchased two loaves of bread at twenty-five cents apiece. The other thought that the brother would be giving him one out of the two, so they would each have one. He believed that his best friend, his fasting partner would share with him. But he realized that the brother began to squeeze the loaves, trying to determine which one weighed more, which was bigger, that he might take it for himself and then give his friend the smaller one. The brother who had no money, upon realizing that, told the purchaser, "You don't have to give me a whole loaf, just give me half." The buyer of the loaves squeezed the bread again and amazingly, he told his friend, "But there is not enough to give." And he ate both loaves; his friend had nothing to eat, and they proceeded to fast.

How do you believe God will view such a fast? Let us not criticize him yet, for this is part of the purpose of this book. I believe that this concept about beginning a fast is wrong. He thought that if he had filled his stomach before the fast it would cause him to stay a longer period before getting hungry again. But that is not so; we don't have to stock up. The body has its reserves; just like the camel stores food, humans do the same, and if we are healthy we can go up to forty days without food. Some of us have never used our reserves because we have never fasted or stayed a day without food, drinking just water. But, like I said, we can stay up to forty days using water alone.

Hunger is not the major problem that hinders us during then fast. Temptation is greater than hunger in a fast. Like I said earlier, there are various types of temptations and they are not necessarily evil. But, you may have to attend to something at home, or you may become physically uncomfortable. Now there are partial fasts as well with great benefits, such as what Daniel had in chapter 10:2-3;

"In those days I Daniel was morning three full weeks. I ate no pleasant bread, neither came flesh nor wine in my mouth, neither did I anoint myself at all, till three whole weeks were fulfilled."

We know the benefits that he received, but the point I am making is that in your fast, there comes a time that hunger actually leaves your body. You may feel weak but not necessarily hungry.

There are times that you may feel a little headache and slight at the beginning of the fast. Some people have spoken about a little stomach pain, but that is all, as the body reacts to not receiving food as normal.

Thomas Eristhee

13
BREAKING YOUR FAST

It is more important to break your fast properly than it is to start it properly. I believe this is where a lot of people get it wrong. Remember, the flesh must not have the mastery over you. You are not a slave to your appetite; you have to discipline your flesh. Many have said that the amount of time one takes to fast should be the same amount of time one takes to get back to normal eating. I agree, except that some of us really should not go back to our old way of eating because our eating habits were wrong. Perhaps after a fast is the best time to correct it. Remember, your body is the temple of the Holy Spirit therefore you must take care of it. Many persons want to fast, but because of health problems they are unable to. We should strive to maintain our health as much as we can.

You must be careful how you break your fast. There are many things that you can use to break a long fast. And anything you use to break a long fast can be used to break a short fast or a partial fast. And by partial I mean the fast where you may have been using liquids, fruits, juices, vegetables or small portions of nuts, as you spent quality time seeking the face of God in prayer.

There are many things that other books and doctors will recommend, but I believe there is nothing better than eating a piece of sugar cane as I break my fast. As soon as I have eaten it I feel strong again. I would also recommend fresh herbal tea, such as mint, cinnamon, and many others. I would not use milk after a long fast. You may use orange juice, but ensure that it is very sweet; dilute it with water and add sugar. If you are using apple juice, I recommend that you do the same thing, for anything sour or acidic can cause much pain to your stomach. During fasting your stomach was empty; therefore you don't want to put anything sour or highly seasoned at that time.

Derek Prince says in his book, Experiencing God's Power, "I have discovered when I have fasted for a long time that my stomach was like a baby's. I had to be as careful about feeding myself after that fast as I would have been feeding a baby. You would be very careful how you feed a baby, therefore be careful how you break your fast. Use the right food and by small quantities and do that over a period of time.

The second day following a long fast, you can eat things like watermelon and have a light soup like pumpkin or spinach. You can also take in non-acidic juices and teas as well. That diet can be continued for a few days. By the way, when I say soup I am not talking the language of the Caribbean. In many parts of the Caribbean when we talk about soup we mean a bouillon with meat and ground provisions etc. that is not what I mean here; I am talking about just the broth. Afterwards you can move on to fish broth, and vegetables and fruits, until you return to your normal healthy eating.

Don't be greedy after you have broken your fast. Many times God speaks after one has broken a fast than during the fast. So you must remain in a state of consecration and prayer, following the leading of the Holy Spirit. Don't allow food to have dominion over you. That does not mean however, that you have to tell everyone who offers you something to eat that you don't eat this and you don't eat that because you just ended a fast. No, you can simply say 'no thank you'. Fasting is not be seen or heard of men, it is between you and God. He will reward you publicly. Don't blow your trumpet like the Pharisees. If you do that you have no reward of your Heavenly Father.

Again I say to you, breaking your fast does not mean breaking your communication with God. Guard your prayer life; spend quality time with God in prayer every day. Many times you have to fast to get a breakthrough in prayer. When you get that breakthrough you must guard it jealously. There is nothing like hearing the voice of God. He is that friend that sticketh closer than a brother. Spend time with that friend and when you shall call, He shall say 'here I am'. Matthew 5:6 says, *"Blessed are they which do hunger and thirst after righteousness: for they shall be filled."*

14
PUT FOOD WHERE IT BELONGS

I have shown you previously some of the trouble that food has caused all over the world. We are in the state we are in now because Eve ate what God said she should not eat. So the first sin on earth came by Satan tempting Eve to eat the forbidden fruit. I want to now continue to show you some of the trouble food has caused on earth so that it will not have power over you. You see, some people will not fast because food has power over them. The Apostle Paul said in Philippians 3:19, *"whose end is destruction, whose God is their belly, and whose glory is in their shame, who mind earthly things."* Whose

God is their belly – whose supreme happiness lie in gratifying their appetites. Their belly controls them, that is their god. That is what they obey. All they make provision for is their belly. They don't serve the Lord Jesus Christ; they serve their belly. They mind earthly things; they set their affection on earthly things instead of on God.

One of the main complaints of the children of Israel in the wilderness was for food. After they had seen all the miracles that God did for them in Egypt and on their way to the Promised Land, including supernatural provision of food, they still complained about food. They remembered Egypt for food they ate there. They wanted to go back because of the food. They forgot about the slavery they were in and how many of their children Pharaoh killed; how they made bricks with straw and cried to the Lord for deliverance. They forgot all of those things; all they could think about was the food they had. God was vexed with them for this kind of mind set. Psalm 78:24-31 says this:

"And had rained down manna upon them to eat, and had given them of the corn of heaven.

Man did eat angels' food: he sent them meat to the full.

He caused an east wind to blow in the heaven: and by his power he brought in the south wind.

He rained flesh also upon them as dust, and feathered fowls like as the sand of the sea:

And he let it fall in the midst of their camp, round about their habitations.

So they did eat, and were filled: for he gave them their own desire;

They were not estranged from their lust. But while their meat was yet in their mouths,

The wrath of God came upon them, and slew the fattest of them, and smote down the chosen men of Israel."

While the meat was yet in their mouths, God killed some of them; the word says 'the fattest of them'. There was no discipline with food.

In Deuteronomy 8:3, and Jesus quoted it in Matthew 4, the Bible says,

"And he humbled thee, and suffered thee to hunger, and fed thee with manna, which thou knewest not, neither did thy fathers know; that he might make thee know that man doth not live by bread only, but by every word that proceedeth out of the mouth of the LORD doth man live."

Jesus quoted this scripture to the devil when he was trying to get him to turn stones into bread. We cannot just eat and not fast; God expects us to spend time with Him in fasting. Now we see here in Matthew 4:4, the same trick that Satan tried on Eve in the garden, he was trying on Jesus. *"If thou be the son of God command these stones to be bread."* But Jesus did not give heed to the appetite for food. There is a time to eat and a time to fast.

Esau sold his birthright for some food. There are many who are selling their souls for food. Some will not serve God because of food. They have not learned to depend on God. You say to them 'serve God', and the response goes like this, "Who will take care of my children? I am not working. Only my partner (common-law) is working and he does not want to marry me. What do you want me to do?" Those persons put food before God.

The birthright carried with it the spiritual leadership. The first-born was supposed to receive double blessing; that is what God says. The smell of food got to Esau. Had there been no food he may not have said, *"I am at the point to die: and what profit shall this birthright do to me?"* He was willing to part with his birthright, something given to him by God, for a bowl of food. He did not value his spiritual blessing. Esau is a type of the man of the flesh; his concern is about earthly things. He believed he would die if he did not feed the food appetite. His appetite governed him. He was not moved by the Spirit, but by the flesh. The word of God calls him a profane person. There are persons who always believe that they will die if they stay a few days fasting without food. The Bible says that we must not be like Esau. Matthew Henry said, "Was it not better for him to die in honour than to live in disgrace?"

Some Facts About Food

The first necessity of life is not food,

but air. You can live for forty days without food, but you cannot live three minutes without air.

The second is still not food, but water. The body is about seventy percent water and so it needs water to survive. That is one of the reasons I say that water should be taken daily during a fast. You should try your utmost not to go over three days without water. In the scriptures, with the exception of Moses, most of the persons who fasted without water fasted for just about three days. I have gone over three days without water, but I believed God wanted me to do that. We are not even sure that Jesus did not drink water during His forty days of fasting. The Bible does not tell us. It says that He did not eat, but it did not say that He did not drink. Now I personally don't believe He drank water, but that's a matter of opinion; the Bible does not state whether He did or not. But water is important for you even when you fast; it helps cleanse the body. So drink water during your fast, unless the Lord is telling you otherwise.

The third necessity of life is not food, but sleep. Your body can last for more days without food than it can last without sleep. There are those who say that one can go three times the length of time without food than without sleep. "J. Christian Gillin, a professor of psychiatry at the University of California, San Diego, conducts research on sleep, chronobiology and mood disorders. He supplies the following answer; the easy experimental answer to the question is 264 hours (about eleven days). In 1965, Randy Gardner, a 17-year old high school student, set this apparent world record for a science fair. Several other normal research subjects have remained awake for eight to ten days in carefully monitored experiments." So it seems that the body can go for about a maximum of about 12 days without sleep, whereas we can go forty days without food.

Food is the fourth essential. Yet, we behave as if it is the first and must be eaten every four hours. But as you know we don't have to. We should not let food be our God

Almost every part of the body takes a rest, except our stomachs. We cause it to work day and night because of our lack of discipline towards food.

Thomas Eristhee

15
INTERCESSION AND PRAYER

In this chapter I want to motivate you to pray and so I will be using some materials that have helped me to pray and fast over the years, including examples from the scriptures. The term 'intercede' means go between. It is going to God and pleading with Him on behalf of others, or based on conditions in the land.

Intercession was and still is a major part of the people of God who prayed and fasted. Moses was one of God's greatest intercessors. We remember after he had prayed for forty days and forty nights when he came down from the mountain he saw the people worshipping the golden calf. God said to him that He would wipe out the people and raise up a great group that will serve him. Moses went back to God for another forty days and begged God to spare the people, and God did. This is great intercession. He fasted so that God would spare the people from death.

We see in the book of Kings, Samuel stood in the gap for the children of Israel. He prayed and God heard his prayer and saved them from their enemy. To Samuel, not be an intercessor was a sin. 1Samuel 12:23 says, *"Moreover as for me, God forbid that I should sin against the LORD in ceasing to pray for you: but I will teach you the good and the right way."* Should we not stand in the gap for others, for our church, for our nation?

E.M. Bounds, one of the writers who perhaps have had the greatest impact on my prayer life said, "Talking to man for God is a great thing, but talking to God for men is greater." We must talk to God for man. And we must do it now, not when we are dead. When we are dead it will be too late; then, we will only see the change we could have brought if we had stood in the gap for men.

Jesus was a great intercessor when He was on earth. He always prayed for His people. John 17:9 says,

"I pray for them: I pray not for the world, but for them which thou hast given me; for they are thine." And again He prayed for those who will believe in Him. John 17:20 states, *"Neither pray I for these alone, but for them also which shall believe on me through their word."*

Paul was a great intercessor and a man who prayed and fasted often. As a matter of fact, the first time Paul had an encounter with God, even before any Christian had come to him, he prayed and fasted for three days without food or water. Acts 9:8-9 tells us,

"And Saul arose from the earth; and when his eyes were opened, he saw no man: but they led him by hand, and brought him into Damascus. And he was three days without sight, and neither did eat nor drink."

So he started his Christian life with a three-day fast. I think this is important because some people say that they are newly saved and so they cannot fast, but the Bible does not teach that. Another excuse people make at times is that they are too old to fast, but again, the scripture notes the following in Luke 2:36-37,

"There was one Anna, a prophetess, the daughter of Phanuel, of the tribe of Aser: she was of great age, and have lived with an husband seven years from her virginity;

And she was a widow of about fourscore and four years, which departed

not from the temple, but served God with fastings and prayers night and day."

The prophetess Anna was 84 years old and the scripture says she departed not from the temple, but served God day and night with fasting. So we ought not to let our spiritual age, nor our physical age prevent us from fasting.

Intercessors make a great difference in the world. Let us read Psalm 106:23, *"Therefore he said that he would destroy them, had not Moses his chosen stood before him in the breach, to turn away his wrath, lest he should destroy them."* Moses saved the nation. Friends, we can impact change in our nation through prayer and fasting. The prayer of one person can make a big difference in the church, family and nation. Why don't you stand in the gap?

John Hyde, 1865-1912, served as a missionary in India. He had difficulties in understanding the Hindi language. That drove him to prayer. He used to spend all night praying. Because he spent such long sessions in prayer, the nationals called him 'the man who never sleeps.' He asked God that one soul would be saved every year. At the end of the year 400 persons got saved. The following year he asked for two souls; 800 were converted. His prayer was, 'Oh God, give me souls or I die.'

Elijah realized that he had a great key; and that key was the key of prayer. He used it to open and close heaven. You possess that same key. James 5:17-18 says,

"Elias was a man subject to like passions as we are, and he prayed earnestly that it might not rain: and it rained not on the earth by the space of three years and six months.

And he prayed again, and the heaven gave rain, and the earth brought

forth her fruit."

He was a man just like you and me, and if he could do it, you could; if anyone has an advantage here it is you, for we have a better covenant than Elijah did.

E. M. Bounds said, "When there is no prayer, when there is no worship of God, the church is a graveyard." The Holy Spirit gives the church life. Through prayer we ask Him to be in charge; we acknowledge our inability but His ability to give it life. E. M. Bounds continues, "God is the center of attraction, and prayer is the path that leads to God. These men do not pray occasionally, not a little or odd times. But they pray in such a way that their prayers enter into and shape their very characters. They pray so as to affect their own lives and the lives of others, and to cause the history of the church to influence the current times." The church must affect the world, must be part of the history of its time, and must be the leading edge of the day; the voice of the church must be heard in the world. But before it can be heard in the world it must be

heard in heaven.

16
WHAT A WEAPON WE HAVE

Prayer and fasting is one of the greatest weapons we have to get the job done. Mahesh Chavda in his book, 'The Hidden Power of Prayer and Fasting', says, "Imagine that you have been using hand grenades of prayer to move a massive mountain of unbelief, hindrance, or demonic obstructions in your life and ministry. When you combine your prayer with fasting, you suddenly drop a hydrogen bomb on the mountain that is blocking your call and divine assignment." He goes on to say, "Fasting boosts the intensity and effectiveness of your prayer at least ten-fold."

All the major church-fathers spent much time in praying and fasting. It was a doctrine among them, but now persons argue whether we should even fast regardless of what the Old or New Testament, Jesus or His disciples had to say regarding prayer and fasting. But we cannot preach another gospel than that which Jesus and His disciples preached. If we do, it will be a fool's gospel, a gospel without authority, a gospel that cannot meet the needs of the congregation, nor the world; a powerless gospel. The gospel we have been given by God is a gospel of power, over all the power of the enemy. Luke says that is one of the signs that shall follow them that believe.

In John 14:12-14 Jesus says,

"Verily, verily, I say unto you, He that believeth on me, the works that I do shall he do also; and greater works than these shall he do; because I go unto my

Father.

And whatsoever ye shall ask in my name, that will I do, that the Father may be glorified in the Son.

And if ye shall ask any thing in my name, I will do it."

The works that I do you shall do also and greater works. That was coming from the mouth of Jesus. It is better that we listen to Him and not man. One of the ways to work the works of God is to believe on His word, do what He says to do. One of the things He says to do is to pray and fast, especially as it relates to spiritual warfare. Have you not realized that one of Jesus' main conflicts was casting out evil spirits out of people? And in Matthew 17:20-21 we read,

"And Jesus said unto them, Because of your unbelief: for verily I say unto you, If ye have faith as a grain of mustard seed, ye shall say unto this mountain, remove

hence to yonder place; and it shall remove; and nothing shall be impossible unto you.

Howbeit this kind goeth not out but by prayer and fasting."

The apostle Paul gives a list proving himself as a minister of God. On that list he mentions fasting often. Not just fasting but fasting often. *"In weariness and painfulness, in watchings often, in hunger and thirst, in fasting often, in cold and nakedness."* (2 Corinthians 11:27). Not just in hunger and thirst when he did not have anything to eat, but when he deliberately stayed without food to seek God. From the book, The Revival We Need, by Oswald J. Smith, he writes, "I do not believe that there is power enough on earth or in Hell to prevent a revival if I am willing to pay the price." Friends, I believe that God wants holy, willing vessels to do His work. If you are willing, hell cannot stop you.

Oswald Smith continues to write, "It is only by waiting before that throne of grace that we become endued with the Holy Fire." They that wait upon the Lord shall renew their strength. We are told that the sun never rose in China without finding Hudson Taylor on his knees. This is what the word of God says in Jeremiah 33:3, *"Call unto me, and I will answer thee, and shew thee great and mighty things, which thou knowest not."* And again in Isaiah 62:6-7 we read,

"I have set watchmen upon thy walls, O Jerusalem, which shall never hold their peace day nor night: ye that make mention of the LORD, keep not silence,

And give him no rest, till he establish, and till he make Jerusalem a praise in the earth."

We are watchmen, we cannot keep silence. We must travail before there is birth.

Isaiah 66:8, *"Who hath heard such a thing? Who hath seen such things? Shall the earth ne made to bring forth in one day? Or shall a nation be born at once? For as soon as Zion travailed, she brought forth her children."*

I have one more important scripture before we move on, and it is a great scripture. Isaiah 64:7,

"And there is none that calleth upon thy name, that stirreth up himself to take hold of thee: for thou hast hid thy face from us, and hast consumed us, because of our iniquities."

Do not let this scripture find its fulfillment in your life. Let it be said of you there is a man that stirreth up himself to take hold of God.

17
CONCLUSION

My friends, I want to encourage you to take praying and fasting very seriously. Now you may say 'Bishop this is hard, I don't know if I can do it'. I believe you can. God will not ask us to do something He knows we cannot do; and besides, He is always there to help us. I believe that everyone that is reasonably healthy can pray and fast. If you are a Christian you should be fasting often because the word of God says "when" you fast not if you fast; also there are great needs in our homes, churches, communities and nation and the world. Individually, we have personal needs we want met as well. I believe one man standing in the gap in prayer and fasting can change the course of a nation, can cause a spiritual explosion, so why not you? If not you, who? If not now, when? It is overdue; the harvest is rotting.

Now even the Pharisees fasted twice a week but for the wrong reason, for they were just religious, not saved. They did it to be seen of men, to receive praise of men, not to help man, not to see revival, not for the furtherance of the kingdom of God. They did not do it to deliver people from demon possession, but just to be seen of men. Yet they were able to fast twice a week. And they did so without the assistance of the Holy Spirit; I say without His assistance because the Holy Spirit will not help you to do something wrong or with the wrong motive.

Physical man has the capacity to stay without food for a long period of time. The children of God have even greater capacity than the unbeliever to stay without food because we have the Holy Spirit who helps us while we are fasting. A lot of people are staying without food for the wrong reasons. Some are spending days without food, seeking the devil for devilish powers and for material things. In the scripture we read of some forty men who made a vow that they will not eat except they kill Paul. Let us read the account in Acts 23:12-13,

"And when it was day, certain of the Jews banded together, and bound themselves under a curse, saying that they would neither eat nor drink till they had killed Paul. And they were more than forty which had made this conspiracy.

I wonder how many people have made vows that they will not eat, in order to stop the progress of your church, maybe to stop you from moving forward. A lot of things are happening in this spiritual dark world. Remember, we are not fighting against flesh and blood but spiritual wickedness in high places. Therefore we cannot fight the devil physically. We need to fight him with spiritual weapons and one such weapon, the mightiest, is the weapon of prayer and fasting. It is like an unmanned drone; you stay on your knees in the presence of God and you direct it with Holy Spirit precision, straight into the enemy's camp. Your prayer always hit its target when it is directed by the Holy Ghost. Why not use it? You don't have to go to the battle field; where you need to be is in your closet with God and He will be on the field fighting your battle. You win your battle in prayer, in the spirit realm, and when you have won it there, then you will have it physically. The fight is in the spirit realm.

You must be willing to make sacrifices

To achieve anything in this life there must be sacrifice. If you are a nurse and you want to go higher, you want to be a doctor, you may have to leave the job and the salary you are getting; you may even have to leave your family for a long time to go to university, maybe for seven years. But you want to become a doctor; maybe it is to help people or perhaps you just want to make more money. Whatever the purpose is, to achieve your objective you must make sacrifices. Sometimes even going to work is a sacrifice. The environment may not be the best; the conditions may not be good. But you need the money to take care of your family so you make the sacrifice until better can be done.

Anybody who did some meaningful work for God made some great sacrifice.

Daniel 3:10-18 says,

"Thou, O king, hast made a decree, that every man that shall hear the sound of the cornet, flute, harp sackbut, psaltery, and dulcimer, and all kinds of musick, shall fall down and worship the golden image:

And whoso falleth not down and worshippeth, that he should be cast into the midst of a burning fiery furnace.

There are certain Jews whom thou hast set over the affairs of the province of Babylon, Shadrach, Meshach and Abednego; these men, O king, have not regarded thee: they serve not thy gods, nor worship the golden image thou hast set up.

Then Nebuchadnezzar spake and said unto them, Is it true, O Shadrach, Meshach, and Abednego, do not ye serve my gods nor worship the golden image which I have set up?

Now if ye be ready that at what time

ye hear the sound of the cornet, flute, harp, sackbut, psaltery, and dulcimer, and all kinds of musick, ye fall down and worship the image which I have made; well: but if ye worship not, ye shall be cast the same hour into the midst of a burning fiery furnace; and who is that God that shall deliver you out of my hands?

Shadrach, Meshach and Abednego, answered and said to the king, O Nebuchadnezzar, we are not careful to answer thee in this matter.

If it be so, our God whom we serve is able to deliver us from the burning fiery furnace, and he will deliver us out of thine hand, O king.

But if not, be it known unto thee, O king, that we will not serve thy gods, nor worship the golden image which thou hast set up."

The Hebrew boys made a sacrifice. Their very lives were in danger but they said they would not obey the king, to bow to his image; God will deliver us, but if not, we prefer to die. And guess what; God delivered them in the most miraculous way. An angel, or Jesus Himself came into the fire with them and the fire had no power over them. We need to read verse 27;

"And the princes, governors, and captains, and the king's counsellors, being gathered together, saw these men, upon whose bodies the fire had no power, nor was an hair of their head singed, neither were their coats changed, nor the smell of fire had passed on them."

They saw these men upon whose bodies the fire had no power. All of Nebuchadnezzar's chief counsellors saw them in the fire and the fire had no power over them. Nebuchadnezzar, the idol worshipper, had to bless the God of Shadrach, Meshach and Abednego. He said there is no god like their God, and nobody must speak against their God. In addition to that, he promoted them. God received all the praise because these men made a sacrifice and they had the greatest testimony of their lives. What sacrifice are you willing to make to see the glory of God? You can start with a few days of fasting.

If you are going to affect the world, you cannot do what everybody else is doing. You cannot be at the same level, you must go a little farther; you cannot be in the outer court, nor the inner court. You must be in the holy of holies as often as you can; live in there. When men are sleeping like the disciples in Gethsemane, we must be praying; while men are eating we must be fasting; while men are satisfied with the usual we must desire the supernatural. We must want what God wants in this world and we must seek Him to see it happen. We must be willing to avail ourselves to be channels that He can use. We must not leave our work for another generation to do for us; we cannot afford to fail. If we do, there might be a generation after us that does not know God. We must fulfill the will of God in our generation. We must say like Paul, *'I have fought a good fight, I have finished my course, I have kept the faith.'* (2 Timothy 4:7).

We want to face our master in the next life and hear Him say, 'Well done thou good and faithful servant.' We must seek to positively affect our generation and the next, even generations that have not been born; we must stand in the gap before God on their behalf. Why not you?

Paul says in 2 Corinthians 4:16, *"...though our outward man perish, yet the inward man is renewed day by day."* This is one of the reasons I say to people, it is much better if you can get out of your home to a place alone with God. Your family may say things like, 'you are getting skinny', or 'I can see all your bones', or 'I think you should stop fasting'. They are only looking on the outward man. Don't be disturbed by those who don't understand the spiritual world. You must have the attitude of Uriah in 2 Samuel 11:11;

"And Uriah said unto David, The ark, and Israel, and Judah, abide in tents; and my lord Joab, and the servants of my lord, are encamped in the open fields; shall I then go into mine house, to eat and to drink, and to lie with m y wife? As thou livest, and as thy soul liveth, I will not do this thing."

This is time that we must be fighting. You must say like Jacob, 'I will not let you go until you bless me'; or say like Esther, 'If I perish, I perish, but I am going to see the king'; or like David, 'Is there not a cause?' you must say like Caleb and Joshua, 'We are well able to take this land'. You've got to say 'if none go with me in prayer and fasting, yet will I follow in this path'.

Maybe one of the areas of your ministry is to minister to the Lord in prayer and fasting; don't run away from it. The Lord will use you to bring light in the darkness. Maybe instead of complaining about all the things that we think are wrong in the church and in the country, if we take time to seek God in prayer and fasting, we will see quick changes. Because truly prayer and fasting makes a difference.

Esther and her friends saved a whole nation and had their enemies destroyed because they spent three days in prayer and fasting. One hundred and twenty thousand people were spared in Nineveh because they fasted for three days.

Cornelius fasted for four days and God caused an angel to bring a message to him. His entire house and his neighbours were saved and got filled with the Holy Spirit. Daniel was praying and fasting for twenty one days and God released one of his mighty angels, Michael, to make sure he received his answer from the Lord. Also, God gave him great insights into the end times that many are still struggling to understand.

To fulfill the mandate God gave us, I believe we need to seek Him in serious prayer and fasting. In the book of Luke 18, Jesus says that men ought always to pray and not to faint. He went on to say, 'shall not God avenge His own elect who call Him day and night?' if we are faithful to God and we pray day and night to God He will reward us. It is recorded that after Jesus' forty days of prayer and fasting, that He returned in the power of the Spirit. May you pray and fast and minister in the power of the Spirit.

ABOUT THE AUTHOR

Bishop Thomas Eristhee was converted in his teens when a young man in his community witnessed to him. He spent several years in the church learning about God and all aspects of church life – teaching Sunday School, preaching at weekly services and serving as the president of the Youth Department.

He then felt the Spirit of God impressing upon his heart to attend Bible School. After a few years of indecision, he decided to heed God's call upon his life. Thomas Eristhee left his small business and attended the West Indies School of Theology, where he obtained a Diploma in Theology. After graduation he returned to his homeland, St. Lucia, in the West Indies, and started to pastor at a Pentecostal church. That church experienced much growth under his leadership.

He has since then gone on to plant four branch churches. He has also written four books; namely *Now You Are Saved, What Next?*; *The Church Revealed*; *Satan Exposed*; and *What Should We Believe, Creation or Evolution?*

Bishop Eristhee received his Bachelor of Arts Degree from the Caribbean College of the Bible International. He also did some studies in Malaysia, and the USA, where he received his Master of Ministry Degree with Trinity Theological Seminary, and his Doctor of Ministry with Covington Seminary.

Bishop Eristhee has also served several years on the General Executive of the Pentecostal Assemblies of the West Indies. He is currently the Bishop of PAWI Saint Lucia district.

Bishop Thomas Eristhee pastors the Victory Pentecostal Church in Saint Lucia, which has a membership of about six hundred (600) persons. He has been married for twenty six (26) years to his wife Midran. They have two children, Shimea and Jeremiah.

Bibliography

1. A Hunger For God, Desiring God Through Fasting and Prayer; *John Piper*
2. But Thou O Man Of God; *Jack M. Wilson*
3. Derek Prince On Experiencing God's Power; *Derek Prince*
4. E.M. Bounds on Prayer; *E.M. Bounds*
5. Fasting, A Neglected Discipline; *David R. Smith*
6. Forty Days Of Scripture; *W. T. P. Wolston*
7. Power-Filled Living. How To Receive God's Best For You; *R. A. Torrey*
8. Prayer: The Timeless Secret of High-Impact Leaders; *Dave Earley*
9. Praying Hyde Apostle Of Prayer, The Life Story Of Johon Hyde; *Edited by Captain E. E. Carre*
10. The Believer's Handbook; *Lester Sumrall*
11. The Hidden Power of Prayer and Fasting; *Mahesh Chavda*
12. The Revival We Need; *Oswald J. Smith*

Made in the USA
Charleston, SC
18 July 2015